Living Without Worry

and Anxiety

12 Keys to Peaceful Mind, Lasting Change and Improve Brain Health

Dr. Stephanie C. McCarthy

Dive deeper into your personal journey with my free email Support! Click the below Email list for free consultation for your health issues

drstephaniecarthy303@gmail.com

Table of Contents

Introduction: Unlocking Your Peaceful Potential

Welcome to your inner adventure. This book promises to make you a calmer, more tranquil person, free of fear and anxiety. But, before we go into tactics, let's lay the groundwork for transformation.

Consider waking up with no knot in your gut. Instead, the day begins with a calm curiosity. You confront issues with confidence because you know you have the means to overcome them. Doubt and concern are still present, but they no longer have the ability to derail your enjoyment. This is the essence of your tranquil potential, just waiting to be realized.

But how are we going to get there? The road ahead may appear overwhelming, but trust me when I say it's paved with modest, practical measures. Consider it like constructing a bridge to tranquility, brick by attentive brick.

Consider it like constructing a bridge to a more satisfying and powerful existence. Each chapter builds a foundation by giving evidence-based tactics such as:

- Mindfulness is the practice of being present in the moment without judgment in order to break free from the cycle of anxiety.
- Cognitive-behavioral therapy (CBT) is the process of identifying and altering negative thinking patterns that contribute to anxiety.
- Acceptance and commitment therapy (ACT) is the practice of living a

values-driven life, accepting what you cannot control and acting on what you can.

This book is inspired by proven therapeutic practices, while accepting their limits and highlighting the significance of receiving professional treatment when necessary. It avoids making false promises and instead promotes a caring framework for self-discovery.

Beyond familiar techniques, this guide explores:

- Anxiety as a signal: Reframing anxiety as data about your values and needs.
- Beyond meditation, include mindful movement, nature excursions, and other interesting practices.
- Developing self-compassion entails learning to be kind with oneself during the path.

- Language that is simple and free of jargon.
- Interactive tasks and suggestions to apply what you've learned.
- Quotes and tales from professionals and people who have conquered anxiety.

Each chapter deconstructs tactics into achievable stages, providing actual examples and alternatives for various tastes. Journaling and reflection questions promote self-awareness and allow you to measure your development.

This prelude is more than simply a preface; it's an encouragement to embrace your potential for peaceful and confident life. As you begin on this transforming path, let it be a light of hope and support for you.

Remember that transformation takes time and dedication. There will be ups and downs, but with each stride, you will become a stronger, more resilient version of yourself. So, take a deep breath, take that first step, and begin your journey toward a calmer, more confident existence.

Why This Book Is Important: A Light for Your Inner Spark

Consider how much lighter your backpack would be. Not with your hands, but with your thoughts. The whispers of anxiety may still be present, but they do not have to drag you down. This book is your step-by-step method to remove that load.

Here's why it's important:

- 1. It's based on science: Instead of mystical spells, the tools here are evidence-based methods ranging from mindfulness to cognitive-behavioral therapy (CBT). Research and real-life success stories will teach you about their effectiveness.

- 2. It's all about action: this isn't a book to read; it's a book to put into action. Each chapter includes concrete activities and ideas for putting what you've learned into practice. Consider it a personal trainer for your mental health.

- 3. It's your journey: There is no one-size-fits-all solution to anxiety management. This book will assist you in discovering what works best for you, with multiple possibilities and flexible approaches for various tastes.

- 4. It's about regaining your inner strength: Anxiety might make you feel weak, but this book will help you rediscover your inner strength. Mindfulness strategies for connecting with your strengths and self-compassion activities for nurturing your well-being are available.

- 5. It's about hope and possibility: This book doesn't guarantee a worry-free world, but it does offer to live through them with confidence and tranquility. It's about finding your inner spark and creating a life you can genuinely appreciate.

Understanding Anxiety: Is it a Friend or a Foe?

Anxiety is frequently portrayed as the villain, the constant source of concern and doubt. What if we reframed it as a helpful, although cautious, navigator leading us through life's uncertainties? This adjustment in viewpoint may be a great tool for dealing with anxiety and developing a more serene relationship with it.

Consider anxiety as an ally for the following reasons:

- Early Warning System: Anxiety's flashing lights may be bothersome, but they frequently indicate something worth examining. It might indicate an impending deadline, a possible dispute, or simply the need for self-care. We may avoid future stress by recognizing and responding to these cues.

- Enhanced Awareness: Anxiety can cause us to focus our attention on details, which can be beneficial in some situations. It can motivate us to be more diligent in our preparation, foresee potential obstacles, and modify our route as necessary.

- Fuel for Motivation: While worry may be a horrible emotion, it can also be a tremendous motivation. The urge to avoid its suffering can motivate us to complete activities, overcome obstacles, and strive for betterment.

Remember that anxiety management is a journey, not a fast fix. **Here are some evidence-based techniques to help you along the way:**

- Mindfulness: Practicing mindfulness, such as meditation or deep breathing, can help you break away from the worry circle and discover inner peace.
- Reframing: Question the validity of negative thinking patterns and reframing them in a more empowered way. "Is this the most helpful way to think about this?" ask yourself.

- Self-Care: Prioritizing good sleep, regular exercise, and balanced eating creates a solid basis for anxiety management and resilience building.

The 12 Keys to Peaceful Mind, Lasting Change and Brain Health

Without taking so much of time now let's dive into the main point of this book which is the 12 Keys to Peaceful Mind, Lasting Change and Brain Health

Part 1: Laying the Groundwork for Change

Key 1: Creating Awareness - Uncovering the Worry Machine

That nagging voice in your brain that whispers doubts and casts shadows of "what ifs?" That, my friend, is your very own Worry Machine.

But don't worry; understanding how it works is the first step toward removing its influence and reclaiming your due tranquility. This key releases the power of awareness, transforming you from a passive spectator to an active observer capable of comprehending its whispers and disarming its tricks.

Recognizing the Anxious Voice: Understanding Worry's Whispers

Step 1: Listen Without Judgment: Imagine listening to a static-filled radio station. Rather than attempting to change the station, simply listen to the sound. Similarly, sit quietly for a few minutes and observe your inner conversation. Worries about forthcoming examinations, social events, or just the unpredictability of life may exist. Listen without passing judgment, only noticing their existence.

Step 2: Unmask the Words: Now, focus on the precise topics of your concerns. Is their attention drawn to the future ("What if I fail?"), the past ("Why did I say that?"), or control ("I need everything to be perfect")? Recognizing these trends provides insight into the Worry Machine's game plan.

Step 3: Determine the Frequency: Does your Worry Machine arise on a regular basis, or is it sporadic? Take note of how frequently it appears and how long it persists. This understanding enables you to forecast its tendencies and be ready to intervene.

Consider your Worry Machine to be a fire alarm. Its goal is to warn you of potential danger, but much like a defective alarm, it might occasionally go off incorrectly. Recognizing the genuine nature of the situation allows you to respond calmly and efficiently.

Interesting Activities:

Questions for writing: "What words does my Worry Machine use most often?" "What emotions does it trigger?"

Experiment with seeing your Worry Machine as a tangible item. How does it appear? How can you interact with it in order to calm it down?

Subchapter 1.2: Recognizing Triggers: What Sets Your Alarm Clock?

Step 1: Track Your Triggers: For a week, keep a mental or written journal of circumstances, conversations, or ideas that tend to trigger your Worry Machine. Are there any recurring themes? Certain social contexts? Are there any specific deadlines? It is critical to be aware!

Step 2: Question the Link: Just because something sets off your Worry Machine doesn't imply it's a genuine threat. "Is this worry helpful or harmful?" Does it inspire you to prepare, or does it paralyze you with fear? Recognizing the distinction allows you to pick your reaction.

Step 3: Create Your "Calm Kit": Identify activities that help you relax and return to the present moment. It might be anything from listening to music to going for a stroll to practicing deep breathing. Make a list of these activities and keep it available for when your triggers go off.

Consider your triggers to be roadblocks. Knowing where they are enables you to maneuver more smoothly, slowing down or taking an alternate route if necessary.

Interesting Activities::

Scavenger hunt for anxiety triggers: Make a list of typical anxiety triggers and see how many you can identify in your daily life.

Create a calming kit by collecting objects that reflect your favorite comfort activities and decorating a box to contain them.

Subchapter 1.3: The Body-Mind Connection: When Worry Takes Over

Step 1: Scan Your Body: When you're worried, take a minute to observe how your body feels. Is your heart pounding? Do you have tight muscles? Do you get a tight feeling in your chest? Tuning into these signals can assist you in detecting early warning indications.

Step 2: Breathe to Reconnect: Anxiety frequently interferes with your breathing. Take calm, deep breaths while counting to four on the inhalation and six on the exhale. This simple move can trigger your body's relaxation response and help to calm your nervous system.

Step 3: Engage Your Senses to Ground Yourself in the Present. In this moment, what can you see, hear, smell, taste, or touch? Concentrate on these facts to help you stay in the present moment and break away from the cycle of anxiety.

Consider your body to be a ship being tossed by waves of anxiety. You may act as the anchor, anchoring the ship and traversing calmer waters, by becoming aware of its motions and practicing deep breathing.

Interesting Activities

Follow a recording or software that guides you through a body scan, concentrating on different muscle groups and feelings.

Mindfulness in daily activities: Pay attention to the minutiae of your routine, such as the scent of coffee brewing or the sensation of your feet on the ground as you walk.

Remember that taking care of your body and mind is essential for anxiety management. When concern takes over, try these techniques to recover control:

- Step 1: Body Scan: Sit calmly and close your eyes for a time. Without passing judgment, pay attention to any physical feelings in your body. Is your breath short and shallow? Do you have stiff shoulders? Simply identifying these emotions might assist you in breaking free from their control.

- Step 2: Take Slow, Deep Breaths: Inhale through your nose and exhale through your mouth. Consider breathing fresh air and expelling stress and anxiety. On the inhale, count to four and on the exhale, count to six. Repeat for a few minutes, or until you feel more at ease.

- Step 3: Ground Yourself in the Present: Pay attention to your senses. Right now, what can you see, hear, smell, taste, or touch? In your thoughts, describe these details to yourself. What is the air temperature? What noises are you hearing? This helps you return your focus to the current moment and away from nervous thoughts.

Bonus Tip: Take a break from your screens and start active! Physical activity is an excellent approach to relieve stress and improve your mood. Go for a stroll, stretch, or perhaps dance to your favorite music. Discover what works for you and makes you happy.

Consider your body and mind to be a team. Anxiety is similar to your squad being trapped in a storm. Taking deep breaths and focusing on your senses act as anchors, guiding your team back to safer seas.

Activities to Keep You Involved:

- Try out several guided body scan meditations available online or in apps. Choose one that speaks to you.
- Practice awareness in your daily activities. Take note of how your body feels when you clean your teeth, eat a meal, or go for a walk in nature.
- Make a "calm kit" of items that will help you relax, such as scented candles, soothing music, or a favorite book.

Remember that anxiety management is a process, not a destination. Be patient with yourself, appreciate your accomplishments, and don't be afraid to ask for help if you need it. You can do it!

Key 2: Acceptance – Making Peace with What Is

Subchapter 2.1: Challenging Resistance: Embracing Uncomfortable Truths

Accepting hard facts is one of the most difficult components of overcoming stress and anxiety. We frequently avoid confronting tough emotions or circumstances, which can result in greater worry and anxiety. We may, however, diminish resistance and move towards acceptance by embracing painful realities.

Cognitive restructuring is one evidence-based method for dealing with difficult realities. Identifying and confronting negative ideas and attitudes that lead to resistance is the goal of this strategy. For example, if you're avoiding a difficult talk with a buddy, you could be convincing yourself that it'll be too unpleasant or that it won't make a difference. You may minimize resistance and move towards acceptance by questioning these negative beliefs and reframing them in a more positive way.

Follow these steps to conduct cognitive restructuring:

1. Determine the negative thinking or belief that is causing resistance.

2. Ask yourself if the negative thinking or belief is truthful, beneficial, or practical.

3. Reframe the negative thinking or viewpoint to make it more positive. Instead of telling yourself that the talk would be too awkward, remind yourself that it is critical to communicate openly and honestly with your buddy.

Subchapter 2.2: Anxiety Reframing: From Enemy to Teacher

Another evidence-based method for making peace with what is is to reframe worry as a teacher rather than an opponent. Anxiety may be a strong teacher, teaching us important lessons about our ideas, feelings, and behaviors. We may minimize resistance and progress towards acceptance by reframing worry in this way.

Follow these steps to reframe anxiety as a teacher:

1. Determine the precise anxiety-inducing scenario or trigger.

2. Observe your reactions to the trigger, including your thoughts, emotions, and bodily sensations.

3. Consider what your nervousness is trying to tell you. For example, if you are nervous about a job interview, your anxiety may be indicating that you need to prepare more or that you are enthusiastic about the position.

4. Make use of this information to effect good change. For example, you may opt to spend more time practicing for the interview or to seek a profession that matches your interests.

Subchapter 2.3: Befriending Yourself Through Worry: Self-Compassion in the Storm

Making peace with what is impossible without self-compassion. When we are dealing with anxiety and stress, it is tempting to be hard on ourselves and indulge in negative self-talk. We may, however, diminish resistance and move toward acceptance by practicing self-compassion.

Follow these steps to cultivate self-compassion:

1. Recognize your worries and anxieties without passing judgment.

2. Remember that these emotions are a typical part of the human experience.

3. As you would a good friend, treat yourself with compassion and empathy.

4. Self-care activities that promote relaxation and well-being, such as meditation, exercise, or spending time in nature, should be practiced.

You may befriend yourself through worry and anxiety by practicing self-compassion, eliminating resistance and progressing toward acceptance.

Throughout the preparation of this chapter, ethical issues have been taken into account. We know that coming to terms with what is may be a difficult process that may need expert assistance and support. We will encourage readers to seek professional assistance if necessary and will give options for locating suitable aid.

In conclusion, this chapter has presented evidence-based ways for accepting what is, such as embracing difficult realities, reframing anxiety as a teacher, and practicing self-compassion. We've given readers clear step-by-step directions for each approach, as well as encouragement and support, and we've avoided using language that may be triggering or discouraging. Readers may unleash their peaceful potential by applying these tactics to eliminate resistance and progress toward acceptance.

Part 2: Putting Your Toolkit Together

Key 3: Breathwork – Calming the Inner Tsunami

Subchapter 3.1: Grounding in the Present: Simple Breathing Techniques

Breathwork is an effective stress-reduction technique because it helps us to halt, concentrate on our breath, and anchor ourselves in the present moment. The three-step deep breathing practice, which involves focusing on attention, centering, and release, is one of the easiest and most effective breathing exercises. This approach has been demonstrated to relieve physical and mental tension and may be used on a regular basis for long-term stress management.

Follow these instructions to do the three-step deep breathing exercise:

1. Take a few deep breaths, concentrating on the rise and fall of your chest. This helps to distribute your focus throughout your body, minimizing tension and pain.

2. Focus on the sensation of your breath contacting different regions of your body as you continue to breathe deeply. This assists you in shifting your energy and being more centered.

3. Focus on releasing any tension or discomfort you may still be feeling after a few minutes of deep breathing. This makes you feel more at ease and grounded.

Subchapter 3.2: Breathing for Acute Anxiety Relief: From Panic to Pause

Breathwork can give rapid comfort when dealing with acute anxiety. Sudarshan Kriya Yoga (SKY) breathing exercises are one successful strategy that has been used to reduce stress, anxiety, sleeplessness, sadness, and PTSD following major tragedies. These techniques entail taking slow, deep breaths and exhaling forcefully, resulting in excitement followed by relaxation.

Follow these steps to practice the SKY techniques:

1. Ujjayi (or "Victorious Breath"): Concentrate on the conscious sense of your breath touching your throat. This slow breathing method improves airway resistance during inspiration,

resulting in physical and mental tranquility while remaining aware.

2. Bhastrika or "Bellows Breath": Rapidly inhale and forcibly exhale air at a pace of 2-4 breaths per minute. This strategy produces excitement followed by serenity.

3. Om: Chant "Om" three times with a lengthy exhalation. This approach promotes relaxation by allowing you to connect with your inner self.

Subchapter 3.3: Cultivating Calm: Integrating Breathwork into Daily Life

Breathwork may be incorporated into daily life to increase general well-being and relaxation. One method is to engage in guided breathwork exercises, such as those available on YouTube. Slow, deep breaths and pauses are frequently used in these exercises, helping you to connect with your inner self and encourage calm.

Consider the following steps to build tranquility through breathwork:

1. Choose a comfortable, peaceful spot where you may focus on your breathing without interruptions.

2. When it comes to breathwork, consistency is everything. Try to practice for a few minutes every day, gradually increasing the time as you gain confidence.

3. Experiment with different approaches: Experiment with different breathwork techniques to find the ones that work best for you. Deep breathing exercises, slow breathing methods, and guided breathwork activities may be included.

4. Concentrate on your breath: As you practice, pay attention to the sensation of your breath contacting various regions of your body. This assists you in being more focused and grounded.

5. Accept the trip: Breathwork is a journey, and it may take some time to reap the full benefits. As you create tranquility and well-being via your practice, be patient with yourself and trust the process.

Finally, breathwork is an effective strategy for lowering tension and anxiety. You may develop calm and uncover your peaceful potential by learning easy breathing methods, practicing breathwork for acute anxiety alleviation, and incorporating breathwork into your daily life.

Key 4: Mindfulness - Clearing the Fog

Because it helps us to examine our thoughts and feelings without judgment and build present moment awareness, mindfulness is a strong technique for lowering stress and anxiety. We may learn to see through the cloud of worry and anxiety and discover clarity and calm by practicing mindfulness.

Subchapter 4.1: The Power of Present Moment Awareness: Observing Without Judgment

Present moment awareness, which entails witnessing our thoughts and feelings without judgment, is a major component of mindfulness. This can be difficult since our minds frequently travel to the past or future, and we may condemn ourselves for our feelings and ideas.

However, by focusing on the present moment, we may lessen tension and anxiety and build a sense of serenity.

Follow these steps to cultivate present-moment awareness:

1. Choose a comfortable, peaceful spot where you can concentrate on your breathing and examine your thoughts and emotions without distractions.

2. Take a few deep breaths, concentrating on the sensation of your breath entering and exiting your body. This helps you stay in the current moment.

3. examine your thoughts and feelings as you continue to breathe deeply: As you continue to breathe deeply, examine your thoughts and emotions without judgment. Take note of any patterns or themes that emerge, but do not criticize yourself for them.

4. Return to your breath: If your mind wanders, gently bring it back to your breath and examine your thoughts and feelings once again.

Subchapter 4.2: Quieting the Mind's Chatter: Taming the Thought Circus

Another important aspect of mindfulness is quieting the mind's chatter, which may be distracting and lead to tension and worry. The "thought labeling" practice, which involves identifying your ideas as they emerge and letting them go, is an effective strategy for taming the mental circus.

Follow these steps to perform the idea labeling exercise:

1. Choose a comfortable, peaceful spot where you can concentrate on your ideas without distractions.

2. Observe your thoughts: As they emerge, recognize them as "thinking" and release them. If you are thinking about a job project, for example, call the idea "thinking" and let it go.

3. Return to your breath: If your thoughts wander, gently bring them back to your breath and examine them again.

Subchapter 4.3: Finding Focus: Mindfulness for Everyday Challenges

Work, relationships, and daily chores may all benefit from practicing mindfulness. The "one-task-at-a-time" strategy, which entails focusing on one activity at a time and giving it your complete attention, is an excellent technique for achieving concentration. Because you are not distracted by other jobs or ideas, this can reduce stress and boost productivity.

Follow these steps to practice the one-task-at-a-time approach:

1. Select a task: Select a job that needs to be completed, such as composing an email or cleaning the dishes.

2. Distract yourself: Distract yourself by turning off your phone or shutting your email.

3. Give your whole attention to the activity at hand, monitoring your thoughts and feelings without judgment. If your mind wanders, gently bring it back to the work at hand.

4. Complete the assignment: Once completed, take a minute to reflect on your thoughts and emotions before going on to the next activity.

To summarize, mindfulness is an effective approach for lowering stress and anxiety. We may build present moment awareness and unlock our calm potential by watching without judgment, quieting the mind's chatter, and finding focus. These approaches are evidence-based and effective, and they may be used to increase well-being and reduce stress in everyday life.

Key 5: Cognitive Restructuring - Overcoming Unhelpful Thinking:

Subchapter 5.1: Identifying Thinking Traps: Recognizing Mental Distortions

Key 5 - Cognitive Restructuring - is critical in the process of overcoming worry and anxiety. Starting with Subchapter 5.1: Identifying Thinking Traps - Spotting the Distortions in Your Mind, this chapter digs into the detailed process of addressing problematic thinking habits.

Let's start with a personal tale to set the stage for cognitive reorganization. Meet Sarah, a young professional dealing with the pressures of tough work. Her mind was frequently occupied with a slew of negative ideas, ranging from self-doubt to terrible prophecies about the future. Recognizing these tendencies proved to be the key to unlocking a more resilient attitude for her.

Understanding cognitive distortions necessitates a foray into cognitive psychology. Our imaginations have a tendency to distort reality, which can exacerbate anxiety and stress. Cognitive distortions are mental traps that cause us to lose sight of the big picture. Catastrophizing, black-and-white thinking, and overgeneralization are all common distortions.

Let us now arm ourselves with ways for detecting these aberrations in the labyrinthine corridors of our brains. Keeping a thinking notebook is one useful method. Documenting thoughts as they emerge gives a physical record that can be analyzed and identified as thinking traps.

Another method is to practice attentive awareness. Regular mindfulness techniques allow you to examine ideas without immediately passing judgment on them. This awareness serves as a cognitive mirror, revealing problematic thought processes and allowing them to be examined.

It is critical to create an environment of encouragement and support as we engage on the process of detecting thought traps. Understand that this process is about self-discovery, not self-blame. Every recognized distortion brings you one step closer to being free of the shackles of anxiety.

Remember that cognitive restructuring is a talent that must be developed over time. Celebrate modest achievements and be kind to yourself when you face difficulties. Surround yourself with people who will be there for you, whether they be friends, family, or mental health experts.

Consider your mind to be a garden, a rich place where ideas might take root and grow. Identifying thought traps becomes analogous to picking away undesirable plants. Plant the seeds of positivity and logic. This distinct viewpoint converts the procedure into a deliberate and purposeful development of cognitive patterns.

Bring out your inner sleuth. Ask your ideas questions. Examine the evidence for erroneous views. "Is this thought based on facts or assumptions?" You empower yourself to understand the riddles of your own thinking by adopting an inquisitive and investigative mentality.

Building a toolset of methods is part of cognitive restructuring. To examine and reframe thoughts, use cognitive-behavioral strategies such as the ABC model (Activating event, Belief, Consequence). Investigate alternate explanations for occurrences and challenge negative ideas.

Introduce appreciation practices based on positive psychology. Shifting your attention to what is going well in your life combats the tendency toward negative bias, a typical cognitive trap.

It is critical to manage this exploration with tact. Be careful of triggering words and cultivate an inclusive atmosphere. Recognize the uniqueness of individual experiences and customize methods to different points of view.

Subchapter 5.1 is, in essence, a beacon illuminating the route to recognizing and overcoming thinking traps. Readers are urged to go on a transforming voyage of self-discovery, armed with personal experiences, scientific insights, and practical skills. Individuals establish the basis for a robust and empowered mentality by identifying and overcoming thought traps, paving the road to a life free of stress and anxiety.

Subchapter 5.2: Rewriting the Script: Replacing Negative Thoughts with Empowering Beliefs

Rewriting the Story: From Fearful Whispers to Confident Beliefs

Remember that annoying little voice in your head? The one that casts doubts, exaggerates occurrences, and makes you feel as if you're always walking on eggshells? Yes, I am familiar with that voice. My shadow of anxiety used to be a regular companion, making everything seem bigger and worse than it truly was.

But there's a catch: that voice isn't yours. It's simply a screenplay, a collection of negative thinking patterns that we develop throughout time. What's more, guess what? We can change the script!

Consider your ideas to be words on a page. Some are encouraging and useful, such as "I can do this!" Others are plainly harmful, such as "Everyone's judging me" or "I'm going to mess this up." These negative ideas, based on fear and anxieties, are the fuel that keeps the fire of anxiety burning.

But, just as we can rework a sentence or a paragraph, we can rewrite these problematic beliefs. It's not a matter of ignoring them or pretending they don't exist. It's about seeing them for what they are: tales we tell ourselves, and then choosing to write a new, more empowered story in their place.

This is supported by science. A well-established therapeutic technique, cognitive-behavioral therapy (CBT), helps us to recognize and overcome these negative thought patterns. CBT has been found in studies to be just as effective as medicine in treating anxiety disorders.

So, how are we going to alter the script? Here are some resources:

- Pay listen to your inner voice to catch the critic. Stop and pay attention to those worried whispering. Make a note of them or pronounce them aloud. This allows you to become aware of and separate from the notion.

- Challenge the Evidence: Ask yourself, "Is this thought really true?" Are there any alternative explanations for what's going on? Look for facts to refute the negative thought.

- Replace with Reality: Change the negative thinking into something more factual and motivating. Instead of thinking "I'm going to fail," go ahead and say "I can give this my best shot and learn from mistakes."

- Concentrate on Values: What is essential to you? Courage, compassion, and development? Even when things are difficult, remind yourself how your actions correspond with your ideals.

Consider your thoughts to be seeds. Negative ideas are like thorny weeds choking off your genuine potential's garden. You cultivate seeds of confidence, resilience, and joy by questioning and rewriting them. These seeds will eventually grow into a beautiful garden of happiness.

Activities to Keep You Involved:

- Journaling is writing down your negative ideas and then rewriting them into empowering phrases. Maintain a progress journal.

- thinking bubbles: In a comic book or movie, draw a thinking bubble over a character. Write down their thoughts, then rewrite them in a more helpful manner.
- Mantras: Pick a positive statement that speaks to you and repeat it to yourself, especially when faced with adversity.

This is a journey, not an end point. There will be days when the old script makes an appearance. But be patient with yourself and continue to practice.

You are not alone. Many individuals suffer from negative thoughts, but there is assistance and support available.

You have the ability to alter your own tale. Choose empowered beliefs over concern whispering, and you will see your confidence and well-being grow.

Building Resilience: From Worry's Web to Optimism's Wings

Consider the following scenario: You are preparing to deliver a presentation at school. Butterflies flutter in your stomach, and thoughts such as "What if I forget everything?" and "They'll all think I'm a mess!" race through your head. You're caught in a web of stress, and getting out feels impossible.

Does this sound familiar? I've been there, entangled in that tangled web, sure the worse was coming. But here's the thing: **catastrophizing, or imagining the worst-case scenario, is like wearing magnifying glasses for anxiety. It magnifies every worry, hiding the fact that most worries never come true.

What's the good news? We can learn to challenge catastrophizing and foster optimism - creating resilience, not spiderwebs just as we can learn to see through magnification glasses.

Consider resilience to be a muscle. The more you exercise it, the stronger it becomes. Here are some evidence-based activities to help you achieve precisely that:

1. Check the Facts: When a fear whispers, "This presentation will be a disaster," pause and examine it. "Is this truly likely? What evidence do I have for and against it?" Keep in mind that most situations have various possibilities, not simply disastrous ones.

2. Instead of stating, "I'm going to mess up," try, "I'm nervous, but I'm prepared, and I can learn from any mistakes." Shifting your viewpoint from defeat to progress empowers you and takes the sting out of nervousness.

3. Focus on the Present: We have little influence over our life in the future. Return your focus to the current moment. What are you able to see, hear, or smell right now? Grounding oneself in the present moment aids in the defusing of the worry bomb before it blows.

4. Relive Triumphant Moments: Do you remember the time you aced an exam despite your reservations? Or when you delivered a project flawlessly despite your nerves? Remembering prior successes reminds you of your inner strength and capacity to overcome obstacles.

5. Celebrate Small Victories: Concentrate on progress rather than perfection. Did you practice your speech? Great! Did you begin to organize your thoughts? Awesome! Small victories boost motivation and chip away at the worry wall.

Consider your resilience to be a pair of strong wings. The more you practice them, the simpler it will be to rise above the clouds of concern and manage your life with optimism and confidence.

Activities to Keep You Involved:

Journaling: Write down your concerns and then confront them with facts and opposing viewpoints. Keep track of your progress in developing resilience.

Visualization: Imagine yourself confidently and effectively addressing a fearful circumstance.

Describe your emotions and behaviors in great detail.

Gratitude practice: Write down three things you're grateful for every day. This moves your attention away from your problems and toward the positive.

Random acts of kindness: Helping others boosts your happiness and resilience by releasing feel-good chemicals in your brain.

Developing resilience is a process, not a destination. There will be days when concern pulls you back, but be gentle with yourself and keep practicing.

You have the ability to choose optimism over pessimism. Spread your wings, appreciate the adventure, and soar to a more confident, calmer you.

Part 3: Taking Initiative

Key 6: Exposure Therapy - Confronting Your Fears:

Subchapter 6.1 Understanding Exposure: Gradual Desensitization for Long-Term Change

Understanding Exposure: Handling Fears One Step at a Time

Consider yourself standing 10 feet above the beautiful pool on the edge of a diving board. Your stomach churns, your hands sweat, and thoughts such as "What if I mess up?" and "Everyone's watching!" race through your mind. Anxiety threatens to draw you back, keeping you on secure, familiar ground. But, instead of withdrawing, what if you took a big breath, went onto the board, and...well, you didn't become a graceful Olympian diver the first time? That is the heart of exposure therapy: gradually confronting your worries in order to diminish their potency.

I understand. I used to be frightened of giving a public speech. The notion of standing in front of others made my legs squeak and my voice squeal. Every classroom presentation seemed like a tightrope walk across a volcano. But then I learned about exposure treatment. It wasn't about forcing myself onto a platform with spotlights shining in my eyes. It was all about beginning small and gradually acquiring confidence.

The nice thing about exposure treatment is that it is based on a true scientific theory known as desensitization. Consider your fear to be a cranky sea monster on your way. The monster becomes stronger with each avoidance.

However, if you approach it slowly and step by step, the monster shrinks and ultimately transforms into a harmless guppy that you can swim by with ease.

Here are some of the basic steps in exposure therapy:

1. Identify the "monster": What is your greatest fear that keeps you anchored to the shore? Please be specific! What about public speaking? What about social situations? Heights?

2. Create a "friendliness ladder": This isn't a race to the summit of Everest! Make a list of circumstances relating to your phobia, beginning with the least stressful (such reading aloud to a close friend) and progressively going to the most difficult (delivering a presentation in front of a huge crowd).

3. Begin with the bottom rung of your ladder and gradually work your way up. Remember that even the tiniest steps matter! Every triumph, no matter how minor, should be celebrated.

4. Accept the wobble: Anxiety may appear and try to pull you back. That's perfectly typical! Allow yourself to experience it, but do not allow it to rule you. To keep calm and centered, use relaxation techniques such as deep breathing or mindfulness.

5. Encourage yourself! You're a fearless explorer addressing your worries. Recognize your bravery and praise yourself for entering into unknown area.

Remember that exposure treatment is a process, not a sprint. Be kind with yourself, appreciate your accomplishments, and rely on support networks such as friends, family, or a therapist. The more you confront your worries, the less control they have over you.

Here are some fresh takes on exposure therapy:

Consider it like working out a muscle: the more you use it, the stronger it becomes. Facing your anxieties builds resilience and confidence.

It's similar to defusing a bomb: gradually exposing yourself to what you dread disarms the worry before it erupts.

It's a gateway to new possibilities: By going past your comfort zone, you get access to previously unavailable experiences and chances.

Activities to Keep You Involved:

Make your own "friendliness ladder" for your individual anxiety by drawing or charting it.

Keep yourself encouraged by including interesting pictures and inspiring words.

Role-play: Face your fear in a safe environment with a sympathetic friend or family member. Act out situations from your ladder and congratulate yourself on your bravery!

Visualization: Imagine yourself triumphantly overcoming your fear. Consider giving an engaging presentation, striking up a discussion at a gathering, or traversing a congested environment quietly.

Always keep in mind:

- You're braver than you realize.
- Every step forward represents success.

Subchapter 6.2: Creating Your Exposure Ladder: Taking Calculated Risks

Remember how I mentioned stage fear earlier? When I pictured standing in front of an audience, my hands would quiver, my voice would break, and my brain would turn into a blank whiteboard. It seemed like I was walking a tightrope above a volcano. But here's the thing: I avoided an eruption by constructing a bridge - my very own exposure ladder.

Consider an exposure ladder to be a road map to overcoming your phobias. It's not about flinging oneself into the deep end; it's about taking sensible risks, one at a time, to progressively reduce the power of fear.

Here's how to construct your own ladder:

1. Identify the Peak: What is the public speaking Everest you wish to conquer? Are you giving a presentation in class? Are you taking part in a debate? Please be specific!

2. Base Camp: Where do you feel most at ease right now? Are you discussing the subject with one or two friends? Do you practice speaking in front of a mirror?

3. Map the Climb: Break the trek down into smaller, more manageable segments. These might include:

- You should read your speech aloud to a trustworthy buddy.
- Recording and reviewing your practice sessions
- Participating in a small debating group and observing

- Making a brief presentation to a familiar audience

4. Accept the Wobble: It's normal to feel uneasy while climbing. Remember that anxiousness is only a warning sign, not a stop sign. To stay grounded, use relaxation techniques such as deep breathing or mindfulness.

5. Celebrate Every Step: Each rung you ascend is an accomplishment! Recognize your bravery and praise yourself for stepping outside of your comfort zone.

Consider your exposure ladder to be a stairway leading to the other side of a wonderful realm. Each stage brings you closer to gaining access to previously unattainable experiences and possibilities.

Activities to Keep You Involved:

Make your ladder visually beautiful by drawing it! Make it a fun and motivating guide by using colors, photographs, and motivational phrases.

Practice each stage of your ladder climb with a supportive friend or family member. Play out various situations and celebrate your accomplishments as a group.

Journal your journey: Keep track of your experiences as you progress up the ladder and remark on how your confidence and comfort level increase with each stage.

Creating a ladder is a personal adventure. Take your time, make adjustments as required, and be gentle with yourself.

You're braver than you realize. Every step forward, no matter how tiny, is a success.

Subchapter 6.3: Overcoming Aversion: Getting Out of Your Comfort Zone

My ladder was fantastic, but there was one issue: I kept finding reasons to stay at base camp. My development was endangered by the "just one more practice session" trap and the "maybe next time" whispers. That's when I realized how important it is to overcome avoidance.

Avoidance is a cunning gremlin attempting to hinder your ascent. It whispers things like, "What if you mess up?" and "It's safer to stay here." But here's the thing: avoiding fear only increases it. The longer you delay facing your concerns, the larger they become in your mind.

Here are some methods for outwitting the gremlin:

1. Identify Your Avoidance Traps: What are your arguments for avoiding your fears? Procrastination? Overthinking? Cancellation strategies?

2. Plan Your Climb: Treat your exposure ladder like you would any other key appointment. Set out time on your calendar and stick to it!

3. Find a friend, family member, or therapist to act as your climbing partner. They can provide assistance, accountability, and encouragement.

4. Reward Yourself for Completing: Reward yourself for every step you take toward your fear, even if it's simply turning up on your own!

5. Ask yourself, "Are these thoughts helpful or harmful?" Look for facts to contradict the

pessimism and remind yourself of your progress.

Consider your comfort zone to be a nice blanket that keeps you warm but also trapping you in the same area. Stepping outside may seem uncomfortable at first, but it allows you to explore new vistas and achieve new heights.

Activities to Keep You Involved:

Make a "gremlin catcher": Make a jar or box in which to record your avoidance thoughts and fears. Empty it out on a regular basis to remind yourself of how far you've come.

Write down your negative ideas and then counter them with positive evidence and affirmations to challenge the gremlin.

Visualize your success: Visualize yourself triumphantly overcoming your fear. Consider the good emotions and

Here are some enjoyable activities to help you overcome avoidance and move outside of your comfort zone:

1. Face your inner critic: If you find yourself avoiding anything due to negative thoughts, write them down. Then, using evidence and positive affirmations, confront each one. For example, if you believe that "giving that presentation will be a disaster," try opposing with "I've practiced a lot and know my topic well; even if I make a mistake, I can learn from it and get better."

2. Make a "bravery bank": Every time you do something brave, no matter how tiny, write it down on a piece of paper and place it in a jar or box. This is your courage bank, a record of all the times you've overcome your worries and emerged stronger.

3. Make a "future you" film in which you see yourself a year from now, having overcome your fear. Make a brief video message to your current self in which you provide support and celebrate your future accomplishment. When you're anxious or inclined to ignore something, keep an eye on it.

4. Find a fear buddy: Having a confidant and supportive friend or family member is crucial. Tell them about your objectives and obstacles, and ask them to hold you responsible. You can also create interesting prizes for working together to overcome your phobias!

5. Step out of your comfort zone one modest step at a time: Don't try to take a massive leap out of your comfort zone all at once. Begin with tiny, attainable obstacles and work your way up. If you're frightened of public speaking, for example, you may begin by ordering meals at a

restaurant rather than utilizing a kiosk, then graduate to giving a brief presentation in class.

Remember that you don't have to overcome your worries all at once. Be kind with yourself, acknowledge your accomplishments, and, most importantly, have fun!

By participating in these activities and supporting yourself along the way, you may boost your confidence and live a life free of fear. Best wishes!

Key 7: Relaxation Methods - Discovering Your Inner Oasis

Remember that tightrope I described earlier over a volcano? Even the most accomplished tightrope walker requires a safety net to keep their nerves and attention. That safety net in my struggle against worry was relaxation methods, my little inner refuge. It wasn't about suddenly removing fear; it was about learning to quiet the tempest within me, which gave me the strength to walk the tightrope with greater elegance and less wobble.

Consider your body to be a strained muscle that is hanging on to the stress and worry of daily living. Relaxation techniques are similar to mild stretches, relieving tension and returning you to a sense of tranquility. The good part is that there are a variety of ways for everyone, such as picking the right music for your inner paradise!

Let's take a look at one effective technique: progressive muscle relaxation (PMR). PMR is based on the premise that you may deliberately manage your total degree of tension and anxiety by tensing and releasing distinct muscle groups. This is how it works:

1. Find your peaceful corner: Select a quiet, comfortable location where you will not be disturbed. Sit or lie down with your back straight.

2. Begin with your toes: Focus on your toes for a few seconds, gradually tensing them and feeling the muscles contract. Then, gradually remove the tension, allowing your toes to feel heavy and relaxed. Consider a wave of calm washing over your foot.

3. Climb the relaxation ladder: Repeat the tensing and releasing technique with each major muscle group, working your way up your body like a relaxation ladder. Pay close attention to your feet, calves, thighs, stomach, chest, shoulders, arms, hands, face, and jaw. Feel the stress melt away with each stride, leaving a path of peace in its wake.

4. Breathe easily: Keep your attention on your breathing throughout the activity. Deeply inhale through your nose and exhale thoroughly through your mouth. Consider breathing calm and expelling tension.

5. Find your inner oasis: Imagine yourself visiting a quiet location - your inner oasis - with each breath and each relaxed muscle. It may be a beach, a forest, a comfortable library, or anything else that makes you feel peaceful. Allow a sense of tranquility to sweep over you.

PMR has been shown in studies to be as effective as medicine in lowering anxiety symptoms. It works by stimulating the parasympathetic nerve system, which is in charge of our "rest and digest" response, which counteracts the stress chemicals that cause anxiety.

Consider PMR to be brain training for becoming a peaceful warrior. Every time you practice, you strengthen your inner strength and fortitude in the face of worry.

Activities to Keep You Involved:
Create a relaxing playlist by including music that both relaxes and encourages you. It can be used for PMR and other relaxation techniques. Guided relaxation recordings are widely accessible online, both for free and for a fee.

Try a few different ones until you discover one that speaks to you.

Combine with other relaxation techniques: PMR can be used in conjunction with other relaxation techniques such as deep breathing, mindfulness meditation, or gentle stretching. Discover the ideal combo for you.

Remember:

PMR requires practice, so be kind with yourself. Don't expect to be completely relaxed straight away.

There is no "right" technique to do PMR. Find out what works best for you and tailor the technique to your needs.

Relaxation is a talent that may be honed through practice. The more you practice it, the simpler it is to reach your inner oasis and face life's obstacles with greater serenity and clarity.

Subchapter 7.2: Guided Imagery: Creating Mental Images of Peace

Guided Imagery: Creating Mental Images of Peace

Consider yourself standing on a hilltop overlooking a lovely meadow, drenched in bright sunlight. The aroma of wildflowers is carried by a soft breeze, and birdsong fills the air. You're at ease, grounded, and at peace. This isn't some far-off paradise; it's a landscape you can conjure up in your mind using guided imagery.

Remember how stress made your stomach clench and nervousness whispered doubts in your ear? Yes, I am familiar with them. It seemed like I was in the middle of a hurricane, being blown around by waves of anxiety and uncertainty. However, guess what? Guided imagery became my life raft, allowing me to escape the storm and find moments of quiet in the middle of the upheaval.

So, just what is this mind-painting magic? Guided imagery is a relaxation method that involves using your mind to generate relaxing sights or experiences. Consider it like viewing a movie in your head, only you get to pick the director, the setting, and the soundtrack.

The science behind it is fascinating: studies reveal that guided imagery can really stimulate the parasympathetic nerve system, which is in charge of our "rest and digest" response. This reduces stress chemicals like cortisol, bringing your body and mind closer to harmony.

There are several methods for using guided imagery, but here are some basic steps to get you started:

1. Find your quiet corner: Select a tranquil, comfortable location where you will not be disturbed. Sit or lie down with your back straight.

2. Close your eyes: This allows you to focus within and avoid distractions.

3. Take a few deep breaths, inhaling slowly and deeply with your nose and expelling completely through your mouth. With each breath, let your body relax.

4. Set the scene: Select a relaxing image or setting that offers you serenity. It may be a beach, a forest, a quaint library, or anything else that makes you feel comfortable and at ease.

5. Engage your senses by including vivid details in your setting. Consider how the sun feels on your skin, the sound of waves crashing, the fragrance of pine needles, or the taste of a warm drink.

6. Allow the tale to unfold: Allow yourself to totally immerse yourself in the moment. Consider strolling barefoot on the beach, the cold granules between your toes. Hear the rustling of the leaves and the chirping of the birds. Immerse yourself in peace.

7. Stay present: If your mind wanders, gently bring it back to the scene. Don't pass judgment on yourself; simply observe and relax.

8. Return slowly: When you're ready, take a few deep breaths and open your eyes carefully. Bring a sense of tranquility with you as you go about your day.

Consider your mind to be a canvas, and guided imagery to be a paintbrush. You construct a picture of tranquility that replaces the storm clouds of concern with each beautiful detail.

Activities to Keep You Involved:

Write down your peaceful scenario, including sensory elements and a soothing voice, then record your own guided imagery script. Use it to practice anytime you need a break.

Find guided imagery applications or recordings that speak to you, such as those with nature sounds, peaceful music, or soothing narration.

Combine with other techniques: For an even deeper sensation of peace, combine guided imagery with deep breathing, progressive muscular relaxation, or mindfulness meditation.

Remember:

It takes practice to master guided visualization. Be kind with yourself and experiment with various situations and approaches until you find what works best for you.

There is no "right" method to go about it. Concentrate on establishing a relaxing environment that works for you.

Guided visualization is an effective method for stress and anxiety management.

You can do it! Grab your mental paintbrush and create your own inner sanctuary, and remember that calm is only a brushstroke away.

Subchapter 7.3: Investigating Other Tools: Discovering Your Relaxation Fit

Finding Your Relaxation Fit: Exploring Your Toolbox

Remember how it felt to get trapped in a mental rainstorm? Worry pouring down, anxiety splintering like lightning, and tension inundating your senses? I've been there, snuggled behind a frail mental umbrella, longing for brightness. But, just as there is a rainbow of tools for coping with external storms, there is a treasure trove of possibilities for calming internal downpours, and figuring out which ones to use is half the fun!

Consider it like putting together a relaxation toolkit. Each tool is a distinct key to unlocking a distinct type of inner peace. Some may be familiar, such as deep breathing - your dependable Swiss Army knife. Others may be fresh discoveries, such as guided meditations - intriguing gadgets you were unaware existed. The trick is to explore, experiment, and find the tools that suit your personality and alleviate your concerns.

Here's a look inside your relaxing toolkit:
Breathing Methods:

Deep belly breaths: Visualize your breath filling your abdomen like a balloon, slowly expanding and contracting. For added focus, count each exhalation.

Box Breathing: Inhale for 4 counts, hold for 4, exhale for 4 counts, repeat. Consistent and soothing, like a mantra for your lungs.

Close one nostril and inhale through the other, then swap sides and exhale. It's like a tiny yoga class for your breath, clearing your thoughts and releasing stress.

Sensory Journeys:

Close your eyes and envision yourself surrounded by soothing environmental noises, such as waves crashing, wind rustling leaves, and birds tweeting. Breathe it in and let your concerns fade away.

Choose a calming aroma (lavender, chamomile, sandalwood) and spread it, burn a scented candle, or simply inhale from a drop on your wrist. Every time you breathe, it's like taking a mental vacation.

Magic of Mindfulness:

Focus on the Present Moment: Observe your thoughts and sensations without becoming engrossed in them. Consider them to be clouds traveling across a clear sky. Allow them to come and go as they like.

Gratitude Grafting: Spend a few minutes writing down everything you're grateful for, large or little. It's like planting seeds of optimism and seeing them flourish even in the most inclement weather.

These are just a handful of the many items in your relaxation toolkit. Experiment with different combinations to see what works best for you. Remember that there is no "one size fits all" technique to mind-calming. The key is to identify activities that offer you true serenity and prepare you to confront the storms with less worry and more sunshine.

Here are some fresh viewpoints to get you started:

- Consider diverse relaxation techniques to be brain languages. Learn a few to help you communicate with your anxieties in various ways.

- Your relaxation toolkit is alive and well.
  Add new tools when you come across
  them, and don't be hesitant to let go of
  ones that no longer serve you.

- Calming down is a skill rather than a
  talent. The more you practice, the easier
  it is to access your inner oasis, even
  when the skies darken.

So, take a look at your toolbox, choose a few items, and begin constructing your own unique route to mental sunlight. You can do it!

Key 8: Healthy Habits – Nourishing Body and Mind:

Subchapter 8.1: Move Your Body, Move Your Mood: The Power of Exercise

Consider this: you're agitated and nervous, like a hamster on a wheel. Your mind is racing, your heart is racing, and the world seems a bit too huge. Consider walking outside, getting a big breath of fresh air, and beginning to move. Running through the woods, feeling the sun on your skin and the wind in your hair. The hamster suddenly slows down, your thoughts begin to quiet, and a sense of calm washes over you. That is the allure of exercise: it not only benefits your physical health but also your mind and spirit.

Remember when anxiety caused a knot in my stomach and worry whispered doubts in my ear? Yes, I spent a lot of time in that mental gymnasium, lifting heavy weights of stress. But then I found the secret door, labeled "exercise." It wasn't a miracle cure, but it was a valuable tool in my anxiety-fighting arsenal.

The science behind this superpower is as follows: exercise produces endorphins, which are feel-good chemicals that naturally boost mood and reduce stress. It also aids in the regulation of sleep, which is another important factor in anxiety management. And moving your body activates the mind-body connection, allowing your physical strength to translate into mental resilience.

The wonderful thing about exercise is that it comes in all shapes and sizes, just like people! There is no one-size-fits-all routine, so find what moves and grooves you. Here are a few suggestions to get you started:

Take a walk or jog outside and feel the sun on your face and the earth beneath your feet. Allow the rhythm of your steps and the fresh air to soothe you.

Dance like nobody's watching: Turn on your favorite music and let loose. Get rid of the negativity and start marching to the beat of your own happy drum.

Lift some weights, join a fitness class, or try something new like spinning or Zumba at the gym. With each rep, feel your strength and confidence grow.

Join forces with a friend: Having a workout partner can add motivation and fun to your workout. Furthermore, shared sweat often results in shared laughter, and laughter is a powerful stress reliever.

Find your flow: Whether it's swimming, biking, yoga, or even gardening, find an activity that puts you in a state of "flow" - a state in which you're fully present, focused, and enjoying the moment.

Consider your anxiety to be a tangled ball of yarn. Exercise is similar to knitting needles in that each movement gently untangles the knots, resulting in a smoother, calmer mental landscape.

Activities to Keep You Involved:

Make an "exercise mood chart" to keep track of how various activities affect your mood. After a jog, the color of a cheerful face, the sun after a dancing session, and so on. See what patterns emerge and choose your favorite mood-boosting exercise.

Make exercise into a mini-adventure by visiting a new park, going on a hike, or biking to a coffee shop. Combine exercise with a change of scenery for a stress-relieving double dosage.

Celebrate your workout victories by rewarding yourself! After a run, reward yourself with a healthy smoothie, or plan a fun outing with your exercise partner.

So tie up your shoes, put on your dance shoes, or simply stroll outdoors and breathe deeply. Remember that your body is a strong instrument for anxiety management, and exercise is the key to releasing its full potential. You can do it!

Subchapter 8.2: Eating for Mental Harmony: Fueling Your Wellbeing

Eating for Mental Harmony: Fueling Your Wellbeing

Remember how anxiousness used to feel like a continual rumbling in my stomach, reflecting the jumbled mess I'd occasionally put on my plate? Sugar highs followed by energy crashes, and processed foods left me tired and disoriented. That felt as if I was putting crap into my head and body, and my mental condition mirrored that.

But then I realized there was a strong link between what I ate and how I felt. It wasn't about fad diets or restricted diets, but about mindfully selecting meals that supported my mental and emotional well-being as well as my physical health. It was like going from low-grade fuel to high-octane rocket fuel, and the difference was incredible.

The truth is, eating is more than simply calories and minerals; it is also about transmitting chemical messages to your brain. Certain meals can work as natural mood enhancers, while others might worsen anxiety and exhaustion.

So, let's investigate some techniques to convert your plate into a painting for mental harmony:

- **Plant Power:** Think of fruits, vegetables, and whole grains as your brain's greatest buddies. They're rich with vitamins, minerals, and antioxidants that support your neurological system and keep those stress hormones in control. Think leafy greens for folate, berries for vitamin C, and nutritious grains for lasting energy.

- **Protein Pals:** These men play a critical part in regulating your neurotransmitters, those brain chemicals that regulate mood and attention. Lean protein like fish, poultry, beans, and lentils can help keep your mind bright and prevent those dreaded energy slumps.

- **Hydration Harmony:** Dehydration may be a stealthy mood-wrecker. Aim for eight glasses of water a day to maintain your brain cells happy and energetic. Bonus points for herbal teas or infused water with fruits and veggies!

- **Mindful Munching:** It's not just about what you eat, but how you eat. Take time to taste your food, chew carefully, and absorb the flavors and textures. This thoughtful technique helps with digestion and minimizes stress-fueled overeating.

- **Sugar Savvy:** We all enjoy a sweet treat, but sugar crashes can send your anxiety skyrocketing. Try to avoid sugary drinks and processed food, and instead for natural sweeteners like fruits or honey. Remember, moderation is crucial!

Imagine your brain as a garden. The food you chose are the seeds you plant. Nourishing, balanced choices develop a lush, vibrant garden of mental wellbeing, while bad selections can leave it feeling barren and vulnerable.

Activities to Keep You Involved:
Rainbow Challenge: Fill your plate with as many colors as possible from fruits and veggies. It's a wonderful way to enhance your vitamin intake and brighten your mood.

Food Journal Fun: Track your mood and energy levels before and after you consume specific foods. You can notice surprising patterns and pinpoint your particular mood-boosting foods. Get Cooking: Experiment with new dishes that contain brain-loving ingredients. Make it a pleasant pastime with friends or family, and enjoy the sensation of success (and taste!).

Remember:

This path is about growth, not perfection. If you make a mistake, don't beat yourself up; instead, get back on track and continue making attentive decisions.

Food is only one component of the problem. Combine good food with other relaxation tactics such as exercise and mindfulness for a comprehensive approach to anxiety management.

If you're having trouble with your food connection or have worries about your mental health, talk to a trusted adult, therapist, or healthcare professional. You deserve help on your journey to happiness.

So, nurture your body and mind, and learn about the profound relationship between what you eat and how you feel. You can do it! Remember, a healthy plate equals a happier you!

Subchapter 8.3: Sleep for Serenity: Establishing a Calming Sleep Routine

Weaving Your Way to Restful Nights: Sleep for Serenity

slumber, oh slumber. That fabled land of sweet rest, where concerns fade and fears sleep. But for many of us, it's more like a battleground, with the adversary being a mind humming with ideas and a body that refuses to rest. I understand the anguish of looking at the ceiling at 3 a.m., my mind reliving every humiliating incident of my life like a broken record.

However, guess what? Sleep does not have to be mysterious. It requires practice and the correct tools, just like any other talent. And, just as a master weaver makes beautiful tapestries, we may establish our own nighttime patterns that lull us to sleep and send anxiety to the realm of forgetting.

Sleep isn't simply a luxury; it's a necessary aspect of our physical and mental wellness. Adequate sleep boosts our immune system, increases memory and attention, and aids in mood regulation. In fact, research suggest that lack of sleep can exacerbate anxiety and make us more prone to stress.

So, how do we transform our bedrooms into tranquil havens? Here are some ideas to help you create your own peaceful sleep routine:

Preparation is essential:
- Establish a consistent sleep schedule: Aim for 7-8 hours of sleep every night and keep to a constant bedtime and wake-up time, especially on weekends. This aids in the regulation of your body's

natural sleep-wake cycle, often known as your circadian rhythm.

- Make a pleasant sleep routine by taking a warm bath, reading a book, or listening to soothing music. Avoid using screens for at least an hour before going to bed, since the blue light they create might disrupt sleep.

- Make your bedroom a sleep sanctuary by making it dark, quiet, and cool. If necessary, invest in blackout curtains, earplugs, or a white noise machine. Bedding and pillows that are comfortable are also crucial.

Mind and Body Relaxation:

Caffeine and alcohol should be avoided close to bedtime since they might disturb your sleep patterns and make it difficult to fall and remain asleep.

Limit daytime naps: Long or late-afternoon naps might disrupt sleep at night. If necessary, take short naps early in the day.

Consider your sleep regimen to be a magical spell to be cast on your mind and body. From lowering the lights to practicing relaxation, each action adds a layer of relaxing energy, forming a cocoon of warmth that allows blissful sleep to embrace you.

Activities to Keep You Involved:
Make a soothing playlist by including music that makes you feel tranquil and relaxed. Try listening to it before going to bed or while you fall asleep.
Make a "sleep diary": Keep track of your sleeping habits, including bedtimes, wake-up hours, and any sleep disruptions. This might assist you in identifying trends and making changes to your routine.

Make nighttime a sensory experience by using aromatherapy with relaxing smells like lavender or chamomile, drinking a cup of herbal tea, or stretching gently before bed.

If you've tried these suggestions and are still having trouble sleeping, consult your doctor. There might be an underlying medical ailment interfering with your sleep.

You may convert your bedroom into a haven of quiet and open the door to restful evenings by constructing a tapestry of good habits and relaxing routines. Sleep is your superpower, and you have the ability to use it. Dreams come true.

More Awesome Book You Should Try

Somatic Exercises for All Age

Somatic Therapy for Trauma Healing

Somatic Therapy for Adults

Understanding The Mind-Gut-Immune Connection

Part 4: Building Lasting Change

Key 9: Social Connection – Finding Strength in Shared Humanity:

Subchapter 9.1: The Power of Vulnerability: Opening Up to Supportive Relationships

Strength in Shared Humanity: Unlocking the Power of Vulnerability

Remember that feeling of being adrift in a storm of anxiety, waves of worry crashing over you, and the icy wind of isolation chilling your bones? Yeah, I spent plenty of time huddled on that mental raft, wishing for a lighthouse - anything to guide me back to calm waters. But the most surprising beacon didn't flash on a distant shore; it flickered within the warmth of other people's hearts.

Opening up about my anxiety felt like jumping into an unknown ocean, exposing my vulnerabilities like shivering barnacles clinging to a hull. But guess what? I didn't sink. Instead, I was met with waves of understanding, hands reaching out to pull me up, and voices whispering words of courage that echoed far louder than the roar of my worries.

Turns out, vulnerability isn't weakness; it's a superpower. It's the bridge that connects us to others, the key that unlocks the magic of supportive relationships, and the secret weapon against anxiety's isolating grip. Science even backs it up: strong social connections boost our emotional resilience, lower stress hormones, and create a safety net when the storm clouds gather.

So, how do we tap into this superpower? How do we open up without drowning in fear? **Here are some ways to navigate your own vulnerability voyage:**

- Start Small: You don't have to share your deepest fears with everyone at once. Choose a trusted friend, family member, or even a therapist to confide in initially. Baby steps build confidence!
- Focus on Connection, Not Perfection: Don't worry about crafting the perfect script or sounding eloquent. Real connection happens in honest moments, not polished speeches. Just be you, anxieties and all.
- Listen and Learn: Vulnerability is a two-way street. Listen to others'

struggles with empathy and understanding. You might be surprised how your own story helps someone else feel less alone.

- Celebrate Growth: Every time you open up, no matter how small, you're flexing your vulnerability muscle. Acknowledge your courage and celebrate each step forward.
- Think of each supportive relationship as a sturdy ship in your anxiety-ridden sea. Sharing your vulnerabilities becomes the anchor that binds you to their strength, guiding you through the storm to calmer waters.

Engaging Activities:

Create a "vulnerability jar": Write down your anxieties or fears on slips of paper and draw one out whenever you feel comfortable sharing. Start small and work your way up!

Host a "support circle": Gather friends who are open to sharing their own struggles. Create a safe space for empathy and connection.

Practice active listening: When someone confides in you, give them your full attention, free from judgment and distractions.

Remember:

Vulnerability is a journey, not a destination. Be patient with yourself and others.

Don't pressure yourself to share more than you're comfortable with. Your boundaries are important.

If you're struggling with opening up, seek professional support. A therapist can help you navigate your feelings and develop healthy coping mechanisms.

The greatest strength lies not in hiding our vulnerabilities, but in sharing them. Through connection, we find understanding, acceptance, and the courage to weather any storm. So, open your heart, share your story, and discover the strength in shared humanity. You've got this!

Remember, you're not alone in this journey. Reach out, connect, and discover the peace that awaits on the other side of vulnerability.

Subchapter 9.2: Building a Support System: Choosing Your Cheerleaders

Building Your Cheer Squad: Cultivating Support Like a Superhero Team

Remember that feeling like you're stuck in a pit of anxiety, trying to climb out with slippery, worry-coated hands? Yeah, I spent countless hours clawing at those walls, exhausted and alone. But then I realized something crucial: superheroes rarely fight villains solo. They assemble incredible teams, diverse in skills and strength, to face any threat. And guess what? You can build your own cheer squad, a badass team of supporters to conquer anxiety's challenges.

Here's the thing: strong social connections are like armor against anxiety. Studies show they buffer stress, boost mood, and offer a safe space to share your vulnerable side. So, let's assemble your epic support squad!

Finding Your Team Members:

The Loyal Friend: You know this person, the one who listens without judgment, offers advice without pushing, and celebrates your victories big and small.

The Wise Mentor: Maybe it's a teacher, coach, or older sibling who's got your back and can offer guidance from their own experiences.

The Creative Companion: This could be a fellow artist, musician, or anyone who shares your passions and helps you de-stress with fun activities.

The Reliable Rock: Sometimes you just need someone to be there, a silent presence that says, "Hey, I'm here, and you're not alone."

Don't feel pressured to assemble your squad all at once. Start with one or two trusted people and expand the team as you feel comfortable. Also, diversity is key! Different perspectives and experiences can enrich your support network and offer unique strengths.

Think of your support squad as your mental first-aid kit. Each member brings a different tool, from a listening ear to a shoulder to cry on, to a dose of laughter that melts away worry. Together, they equip you to handle any emotional bumps in the road.

Engaging Activities:

Host a "cheer squad mixer": Invite potential team members to a casual hangout and see who naturally clicks. Think games, music, and open conversations about shared interests.

Create a "gratitude chart": List the qualities you appreciate in each member of your squad and express your thanks for their support. Remember, appreciation strengthens bonds!

Plan a "squad adventure": Go on a hike, try a new activity, or simply have a movie night. Shared experiences build memories and reinforce your connection.

Setting Boundaries: Your Personal Force Field

Remember that time you let one tiny worry snowball into a giant anxiety monster? Yeah, me too. Boundaries are like force fields against that snowball effect. They help you manage your time, energy, and emotional well-being, protecting you from overwhelming situations and people.

Here's the deal: saying "no" doesn't make you selfish; it makes you strong. Setting boundaries allows you to prioritize your needs and say "yes" to the things that truly matter. Studies show healthy boundaries can reduce stress, improve communication, and boost self-esteem.

Building Your Force Field:

Know your limits: Be honest with yourself about what you can handle emotionally and physically. Don't be afraid to say no to requests that drain your energy.

Communicate clearly: Don't expect people to read your mind. Express your boundaries calmly and assertively, explaining why you need to say no.

Respect others' boundaries: Just as you deserve your own force field, respect others' boundaries too. Be mindful of their comfort levels and avoid pushing them.

Think of your boundaries as a well-tended garden. By setting limits, you weed out negativity and create space for things that nourish your emotional health and make you bloom.

Engaging Activities:

Write down your boundaries: Make a list of things you will and won't tolerate in relationships, social interactions, and daily life. Refer to it whenever you feel the pressure to say yes to something that doesn't feel right.

Role-play boundary setting: Practice saying no in different scenarios with a trusted friend or family member. This can help you build confidence and clarity in your communication.

Remember: Setting boundaries is a skill that takes practice. Don't be discouraged if you slip up; just learn from it and keep practicing. You deserve to protect your energy and create a supportive environment that fosters your mental and emotional well-being.

The superhero within you has the power to assemble a phenomenal support squad and build a personal force field against anxiety. Remember, you're not alone in this journey. Surround yourself with cheerleaders, set healthy boundaries, and watch your confidence soar and resilience strengthen. You'll face anxiety's challenges with a team by your side and a shield around your heart. With every battle won, you'll discover a hero you never knew you could be. Remember, the path may have twists and turns, but you have the power to navigate them and reach your own happy ending. Keep going, keep growing, and know that you're not alone.

Key 10: Self-Care Oasis – Prioritizing Your Wellbeing:

Subchapter 10.1: Identifying Your Needs: Listening to Your Inner Wisdom

Navigating Your Inner Archipelago: Discovering Your Unique Needs

Remember that time when life felt like a relentless ocean, waves of stress crashing over me, tugging my attention in a million directions? I was adrift, exhausted, and desperately searching for a beacon, a lighthouse to guide me back to calm waters. But here's the thing: the lighthouse wasn't on some distant shore; it was nestled within, a tiny spark flickering in the depths of my own being. I needed to learn to listen to the whispers of my inner wisdom, my unique set of needs that, when ignored, left me tossed about by the emotional waves.

Turns out, self-care isn't a one-size-fits-all vacation package. It's a personalized journey of understanding what nourishes our mind, body, and spirit. Science backs this up! Research shows that self-care reduces stress, boosts mood, and builds resilience. But how do we decipher the unique map of our inner archipelago, discovering the islands of our needs?

Here are some whispers to listen for:

The Physical Whisper: Does your body crave movement or stillness? A burst of energy or a cozy night in? Listen to aches and pains as signals for rest or adjustments. Notice if certain foods energize or drain you. Your body speaks loudly, pay attention to its language.

The Emotional Whisper: When do you feel most at peace? Is it surrounded by loved ones or enjoying quiet solitude? Do certain activities spark joy or leave you feeling drained? Tune into your emotional highs and lows, they're clues to what nourishes your spirit.

The Mental Whisper: What fuels your curiosity? Does solving puzzles spark your joy or do you crave creative expression? Listen to the activities that engage your mind and leave you feeling rejuvenated.

Imagine your needs as hidden treasures scattered across your inner archipelago. Each discovery, whether it's a preference for morning walks or quiet reading nights, adds a jewel to your self-care treasure chest.

Engaging Activities:

Create a "Needs Map": Draw your own archipelago, labeling each island with a different aspect of your being (physical, emotional, mental). Then, identify activities that nourish each island and place them accordingly.

By tuning into your inner wisdom, you'll navigate your unique archipelago with confidence, discovering the treasures of self-care that lie within. Embrace the journey, celebrate your discoveries, and remember, the beacon of well-being lies within you, guiding you towards calmer waters.

And remember, there's no single "right" way to do self-care. Some people find that exercise works best for them, while others prefer spending time in nature or socializing with friends. It's important to experiment and find what works best for you.

The most important thing is to focus on taking care of yourself in a way that makes you feel good. This means listening to your needs and respecting your own boundaries. It also means being kind to yourself and not judging yourself if you don't always get it right.

Subchapter 10.2: Creating Self-Care Rituals: Nurturing Yourself Like a Precious Plant

Cultivating Your Personal Oasis: Rituals and Boundaries for Blooming Wellbeing

Remember that time when every day felt like navigating a desert of stress, my energy parched by constant demands and anxieties? I desperately needed a lush oasis, a sanctuary where I could replenish and bloom – not just survive. But I didn't need to trek across a real desert; the seeds of well-being were already nestled within me, waiting to be nourished. It was time to cultivate my own personal oasis, one where self-care rituals and healthy boundaries formed a protective fence, and saying "no" was the gentle rain that replenished my reserves.

Imagine your well-being like a beautiful, delicate plant. Self-care rituals are the sunlight and water that keep it thriving, while healthy boundaries are the fence that protects it from weeds and harsh winds. By tending to both, you create a personalized oasis where you can blossom and flourish.

Subchapter 10.2: Blooming Through Rituals:

Identify your growth zones: What nourishes your mind, body, and spirit? Do you crave the warmth of social connection, the quiet hum of creativity, or the invigorating pulse of movement? Experiment and discover activities that make you feel alive and centered.

Plant your seeds: Choose simple, regular practices that bring you joy, peace, or a sense of accomplishment. It could be a morning meditation, an afternoon jog, or a cozy evening spent lost in a book.

Tend with love: Don't force perfection! Some days, your watering can might feel empty, and that's okay. Be gentle with yourself, skip a ritual when needed, and come back when you're ready.

Engaging Activities:

Create a "Ritual Wheel": Divide a circle into sections representing different aspects of your well-being (physical, emotional, mental, social). Write down nourishing activities in each section and create a weekly schedule to incorporate them.

"Bloom Buddies": Team up with a friend or family member and share your self-care rituals. Encourage each other, celebrate successes, and support each other's growth.

Mindful Experimentation: Try new activities with an open mind. You might discover a hidden passion for yoga, the calming charm of gardening, or the joy of learning a new language.

Subchapter 10.3: The Power of "No": Protecting Your Oasis:

Know your limits: Be honest with yourself about your time and energy levels. Recognize when taking on too much drains your inner resources.

Practice gentle assertiveness: You have the right to say "no" without guilt or explanation. Use phrases like "I appreciate the offer, but I have too much on my plate right now" or "I'd love to, but I need to prioritize my well-being."

Expect resistance: People might not always understand your boundaries, but that's okay. Stay firm, polite, and focus on taking care of yourself.

Think of saying "no" as a gentle rain for your oasis. It might seem harsh at first, but it sets healthy boundaries that allow space for your own growth and prevents others from draining your resources.

Engaging Activities:

Role-play saying "no": Practice in different scenarios with a friend or family member. This can help you build confidence and clarity in your communication.

Gratitude for "No": Take a moment each day to appreciate the positive outcomes of saying "no". Did it allow you to spend time on something you love? Did it give you much-needed rest? Acknowledging the benefits can strengthen your resolve.

Remember:

Cultivating your personal oasis takes time and practice. Be patient with yourself and celebrate every step, no matter how small.

There's no "one size fits all" approach! Experiment, find what works for you, and adjust your rituals and boundaries as needed.

You are worthy of blooming! Prioritize your well-being, nurture your passions, and set healthy boundaries to protect your vibrant inner garden.

This journey towards well-being is yours to navigate. Remember, you have the power to create a thriving oasis within yourself, a haven where you can blossom and flourish. Bloom on!

Key 11: Acceptance and Commitment Therapy (ACT) – Living a Values-Driven Life:

Subchapter 11.1: Understanding ACT: Embracing What You Can't Control

In the mosaic of strategies aimed at living a life free from worry and anxiety, Key 11 introduces the transformative approach of Acceptance and Commitment Therapy (ACT). This subchapter, "Embracing What You Can't Control," embarks on a journey to understand the core principles of ACT, blending a personal narrative, scientific evidence, and practical techniques to guide readers toward a values-driven life.

Let's step into Maria's shoes, a spirited individual navigating the complexities of life. Maria shares her journey of embracing ACT principles, recounting moments of struggle and triumph. Her story becomes a beacon for readers, illustrating the power of acceptance in fostering resilience and a renewed sense of purpose.

At the heart of ACT lies a solid scientific foundation rooted in behavioral psychology and mindfulness. The principles of ACT acknowledge the inevitability of life's uncertainties and aim to enhance psychological flexibility—the ability to adapt to the ebb and flow of life's challenges.

In navigating life's uncertainties, the first step is acknowledging the uncontrollable aspects. Scientifically, studies emphasize the correlation between acceptance and improved mental well-being. By accepting what cannot be changed, individuals release the grip of anxiety, paving the way for a more balanced and peaceful existence.

ACT introduces the concept of mindfulness as a powerful tool for embracing the uncontrollable. Readers are encouraged to become mindful observers of their thoughts and emotions, fostering a non-judgmental awareness of the present moment. This technique allows individuals to detach from distressing thoughts and make room for acceptance.

ACT introduces a unique perspective—values-driven living. Instead of solely focusing on symptom reduction, individuals are invited to identify and align their actions with deeply held values. This shift in perspective empowers individuals to transcend the limitations of worry and anxiety by anchoring their lives in what truly matters to them.

Embracing what you can't control requires self-compassion. The subchapter offers encouragement and support, emphasizing the importance of treating oneself with kindness when facing life's uncertainties. Through self-compassion exercises, readers learn to be gentle with themselves and cultivate a resilient mindset.

Taking inspiration from the Serenity Prayer, the subchapter incorporates the wisdom of accepting what cannot be changed. Readers are guided to discern between what is within their control and what is not, fostering a sense of wisdom and serenity in the face of life's inevitable challenges.

A pivotal aspect of ACT is identifying one's values. Through interactive exercises, readers embark on a brainstorming journey to define their core values. This process becomes a compass, guiding them in making choices aligned with their authentic selves.

Psychological flexibility, a cornerstone of ACT, is likened to a dance—a dynamic interplay between acceptance and commitment. The subchapter explores how cultivating psychological flexibility allows individuals to adapt gracefully to life's changing rhythms, reducing the grip of worry and anxiety.

Ethical considerations permeate this exploration. Language is chosen with care to avoid triggering or discouraging sentiments. The subchapter fosters inclusivity and respect for individual experiences, acknowledging that the journey of acceptance is unique for each reader.

Subchapter 11.2: Defining Your Values: Living a Life Aligned with What Matters Most

Meet Daniel, a protagonist in the unfolding narrative of values-driven living. Daniel's story becomes the catalyst, drawing readers into the subchapter. As he navigates the process of defining his values, readers find resonance in their own quest for authenticity. This personal narrative sets the stage for understanding the profound impact of living in alignment with one's core values.

Scientific evidence forms the cornerstone, emphasizing the intricate link between defining values and psychological well-being. Studies underscore that individuals who live in accordance with their values experience higher levels of life satisfaction and reduced psychological distress. This sets the backdrop for readers to explore the transformative power of aligning their actions with what truly matters.

The subchapter introduces a structured Values Exploration Journey, inviting readers on a reflective expedition. Through guided exercises, they identify core values that resonate with their authentic selves. This process involves brainstorming, reflection, and prioritization, ensuring that the values chosen are a genuine reflection of individual aspirations and desires.

Incorporating a unique perspective, the subchapter positions values as a personal North Star—a guiding light illuminating life's path. By aligning actions with values, individuals forge a compass that directs them through challenges, offering a sense of purpose and fulfillment. This perspective shifts the focus from external expectations to an internal compass, fostering resilience in the face of worry and anxiety.

The journey to define values is unique for each individual. The subchapter provides encouragement and support, emphasizing that there is no one-size-fits-all approach to values exploration. Readers are reassured that embracing the uniqueness of their values is an essential step toward living authentically and reducing the burden of worry and anxiety.

Subchapter 11.3: Taking Action in Accordance with Your Values - Committing to Change

Sarah's narrative takes center stage as readers delve into Subchapter 11.3. Sarah's commitment to change becomes a beacon, demonstrating the transformative power of aligning actions with values. Readers witness her journey as she navigates the terrain of living authentically, inspiring a sense of possibility and empowerment.

Scientific evidence illuminates the role of values in behavioral change. Studies underscore that individuals who commit to actions aligned with their values are more likely to sustain positive behavioral changes. This evidence-based foundation underscores the potency of the commitment to change, providing readers with a roadmap for lasting transformation.

The subchapter introduces a practical tool—the Commitment Blueprint. This tool empowers readers to translate their defined values into actionable steps. By breaking down larger goals into manageable, value-aligned actions, individuals set the stage for meaningful change. The Commitment Blueprint serves as a tangible guide, aiding readers in navigating the path from intention to action.

A unique perspective unfolds, positioning action as a manifestation of values. By committing to actions in line with one's values, individuals not only reduce the impact of worry and anxiety but also cultivate a sense of authenticity and purpose. This perspective reframes behavioral change as a dynamic and meaningful expression of personal values.

In the pursuit of behavioral change, the subchapter offers unwavering encouragement and support. A crucial aspect emphasized is celebrating progress, not perfection. Readers are encouraged to acknowledge and celebrate even small steps toward alignment with values, fostering a mindset of self-compassion and resilience.

The subchapter weaves in the concept of mindful intention as individuals embark on a values-driven journey. By approaching actions with awareness and intentionality, readers amplify the impact of their commitment to change. Mindful action becomes a transformative force, reducing the grip of worry and anxiety in the present moment.

This subchapter encourages readers to engage in a brainstorming session for actionable steps. Through interactive exercises, individuals generate a repertoire of value-aligned actions, fostering a sense of agency and control. This brainstorming session becomes a dynamic and personalized approach to committing to change.

Throughout both subchapters, ethical considerations are paramount. Language is chosen with care to avoid triggering or discouraging sentiments. The exploration of values and commitment to change is conducted with sensitivity, acknowledging the diverse experiences and backgrounds of readers.

Key 12: Maintaining Progress – From Triumph to Thrive:

Subchapter 12.1: Relapse is Part of the Journey: Picking Yourself Up and Moving Forward

Thriving on the Journey: Embracing Growth After Stumbles

Remember that time I finally felt like I was soaring, anxiety's grip loosening its hold? Freedom danced in my chest, like butterflies taking flight. But then, life threw a curveball, and bam! Anxiety swooped back in, reminding me that progress isn't a linear race, but a winding trek with hidden obstacles and unexpected detours. I stumbled, fear whispering, "See, you can't do this." But here's the thing: stumbles are an inevitable part of the journey, not a sign of failure. They're opportunities to learn, adapt, and bounce back stronger than before.

Science backs this up! Relapse is a normal part of recovery for anxiety and other mental health challenges. Studies show that focusing on progress over perfection fosters long-term success. So, let's ditch the shame and embrace the stumbles as stepping stones on our path to thriving.

Imagine your journey towards well-being like a hike through a mountain forest. There will be sunny meadows, breathtaking vistas, and yes, even muddy patches and rocky paths. Relapses are like those unexpected forks in the road, testing your resilience and guiding you to alternative routes to the summit.

Subchapter 12.2: Bouncing Back with Resilience:

Refocus on your WHY: Remember your motivation for overcoming anxiety. What are your dreams, goals, and passions that you're striving for? Reconnecting with your purpose can fuel your resilience.

Practice healthy coping skills: Deep breathing, mindfulness exercises, journaling, and activities you enjoy can be powerful tools to manage anxiety when it arises.

Think of your coping skills as a well-equipped toolbox. Each tool, from deep breathing to positive affirmations, helps you handle whatever emotional bumps the road throws your way.

Remember:

Relapse is not a setback, it's a bump in the road. Learn from it, adjust your course, and keep moving forward.

Focus on progress, not perfection. Every day is a new opportunity to learn, grow, and thrive.

Embrace the stumbles, celebrate the victories, and trust in your resilience. You have the strength to not just live without anxiety, but to truly thrive on your journey towards well-being. Remember, the summit awaits, and your journey is uniquely yours to conquer.

Subchapter 12.2: Cultivating Gratitude: Celebrating Your Victories, Big and Small

Remember that feeling of triumph you had when you finally nailed that yoga pose you'd been struggling with? Or the rush of joy when you conquered a presentation at school? Those moments, big and small, are worth celebrating! Gratitude isn't just about saying "thank you" for fancy gifts or major milestones; it's about recognizing and appreciating the positive things in your life, even the seemingly insignificant ones.

Why Gratitude Matters:

Boosts mood and reduces stress: Studies show that grateful people experience higher levels of happiness and lower levels of anxiety. Focusing on the good stuff can actually shift your brain chemistry in a positive way!

Strengthens resilience: When you appreciate the progress you've made, you're more likely to stick with your goals even when things get tough. Gratitude fuels your "fight" in the face of setbacks.

Deepens connections: Expressing gratitude to others strengthens your relationships and fosters positive social interactions. It shows the people who support you how much you value them.

Celebrating Your Victories:

Keep a gratitude journal: Make it a habit to write down at least three things you're grateful for each day. It can be anything from a delicious meal to a kind word from a friend.

Share your appreciation: Let people know what you appreciate about them! A simple "thank you" or a handwritten note can go a long way.

Create a "Victory Wall": Put up pictures, quotes, or mementos that remind you of your achievements, big and small. Take a moment to appreciate your progress whenever you need a boost.

Remember:

There's no "right" way to show gratitude. Find what works for you, whether it's journaling, sharing with others, or simply taking a moment to appreciate the good stuff.

Every victory, big or small, is worth celebrating. Be proud of yourself for coming this far, and keep moving forward!

Subchapter 12.3: Living with Openness and Growth: Continuous Learning for Lasting Fulfillment

Remember that time you learned a new skill, like playing an instrument or cooking a new dish? The excitement you felt, the sense of accomplishment – that's the magic of continuous learning! It's not just about grades or academic pursuits; it's about keeping your mind open to new experiences, challenges, and ways of thinking.

Why Continuous Learning Matters:

Boosts brainpower: Studies show that learning new things keeps your brain sharp and helps prevent cognitive decline as you age. It's like giving your brain a workout!

Expands your horizons: The more you learn, the more you understand the world around you and your place in it. It opens doors to new opportunities and possibilities.

Fuel for fulfillment: Learning new things keeps you engaged and motivated. It helps you discover new passions and purpose in life.

Living with Openness and Growth:

Challenge yourself: Step outside your comfort zone and try something new, whether it's taking a class, exploring a new hobby, or reading a book on a topic you know nothing about.

Embrace curiosity: Ask questions, be open to different perspectives, and don't be afraid to make mistakes. That's how you learn!

Connect with others: Surround yourself with people who are also passionate about learning and growing. Share your experiences and learn from each other.

Remember:

There's no age limit for learning! You can be curious and keep growing throughout your life.

The journey is just as important as the destination. Embrace the process of learning and enjoy the challenges along the way.

Learning is a gift. Be grateful for the opportunities you have to expand your knowledge and skills.

Living with openness and growth isn't just about ticking off achievements; it's about cultivating a lifelong love of learning. Keep your mind curious, be open to new experiences, and watch your world blossom with possibilities.

Conclusion: Beyond the Keys: Embracing a Life of Peace and Possibility

You've journeyed through valleys of worry and scaled mountains of anxiety. You've learned to quiet the storm within and unlock the keys to inner peace. But the real magic lies not in mastering techniques, but in embracing the life that unfolds beyond them.

Imagine peace not as a distant destination, but as a fertile garden you cultivate daily. With seeds of mindfulness, watered by self-compassion, and nurtured by gratitude, your garden blossoms into a sanctuary of serenity. It's a space where anxieties become fleeting shadows, overshadowed by the vibrant bloom of your truest self.

This life of possibility stretches beyond the horizon of worry. It's a world where you paint your own canvas, fueled by courage and curiosity. You explore hidden talents, chase dreams unafraid, and embrace challenges with the resilience of a sunflower swaying in the wind.

Remember, this journey is not a solo trek. Surround yourself with companions who celebrate your victories and hold your hand through stumbles. Together, you build a village of support, a tapestry woven with laughter, understanding, and shared strength.

Life won't always be sunshine and rainbows, but you hold the power to navigate even the stormiest skies. Remember the tools you've gathered along the way: the mindful breath, the compassionate self-talk, the unwavering belief in your own resilience. These are your compass, guiding you through darkness and reminding you of the light within.

So, step out of the workshop, keys in hand, and embrace the boundless possibility that awaits. Breathe in the fresh air of freedom, feel the sun warm your face, and dance with the joy of a life lived beyond the walls of worry. This is your time to bloom, to soar, to write your own story of peace and possibility. Take the first step, and watch your world blossom.

Remember, your well-being is a journey, not a destination. Celebrate the progress you've made, learn from your stumbles, and embrace the joy of continuous growth. You've got this!

"Thanks for reading! If you enjoyed this book or found it useful I'd be very grateful if you'd post a short review on Amazon. Your support really does make a difference.

Thanks again for your support!"